Elijah Irving

GRATITUDE

JOURNAL

FOR

KIDS

Library of Congress
Cataloging-in-Publication Data
Morgan, Priscilla
Gratitude Journal for Kids/ Priscilla Morgan
p. cm.
Illustrated by Simonne-Anais Clarke and Zachary-Michael Clarke
ISBN-13: 9781948071390 (paperback)
Title I.
2019

www.laurensimonepubs.com
laurensimonepubs@gmail.com
@laurensimonepubs

TABLE OF CONTENTS

LIFE GOALS

"Many of life's failures are people who did not realize how close they were to success when they gave up."
Thomas A. Edison

1. What kind of person do you want to be when you grow up?
    _____
    _____
    _____

2. What kind of jobs or careers do you imagine for yourself?
    _____
    _____
    _____

3. Where do you want to live? In the city, by the ocean, or in the mountains
    _____
    _____
    _____

4. What things will you do to stay healthy, active and smart?
    _____
    _____
    _____

5. Where will you volunteer your time and share your money?
    _____
    _____
    _____

6. How will you make the world a better, safer, or cleaner place to live?
    _____
    _____
    _____

AFFIRMATIONS

Choose at least one below and repeat 3 times when you wake up and before bedtime every day.

"I love myself"

"I am enough, and I have enough"

"I am strong, courageous and disciplined"

"I will remain focus no matter the challenge. I will accomplish my goals"

"I am bold and beautiful"

"I am alive and well"

"I am young with big dreams that I must accomplish"

"I feel super fantastic and I believe something great is going to happen to me today"

"I live with purpose"

"I aspire to make a positive difference"

"I am whole, faithful, loyal and trustworthy"

"If you fail to plan, you plan to fail."
Benjamin Franklin

Month: _____

Week: ___

What are you grateful for today?

_____
_____
_____

Week: ___

What are you grateful for today?

_____
_____
_____

Week: ___

What are you grateful for today?

_____
_____
_____

Week: ___

What are you grateful for today?

_____
_____
_____

How are you feeling?

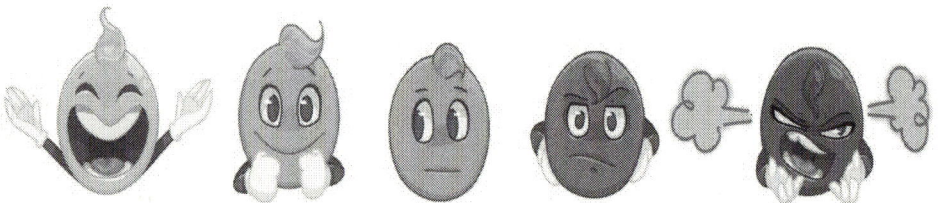

Monthly Reflection

"You're braver than you believe, and stronger than you seem, and smarter than you think." A.A. Milne & Christopher Robin

What was your best experience for the month?

_____

_____

_____

What was your worst experience for the month?

_____

_____

_____

What were you mostly grateful for this month?

_____

_____

_____

What can I do to improve myself this month?

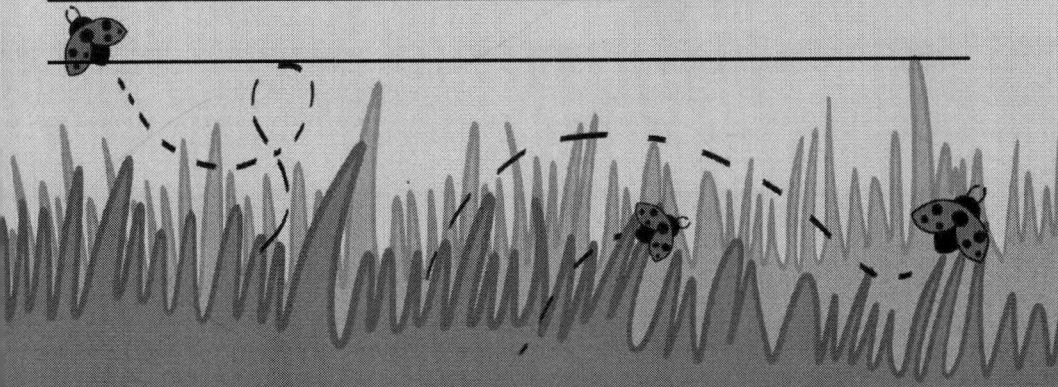

_____

_____

_____

"If you think you can't, then you can't."
Henry Fond

Month: _____

Week: ___

What are you grateful for today?

_____
_____
_____

Week: ___

What are you grateful for today?

_____
_____
_____

Week: ___

What are you grateful for today?

_____
_____
_____

Week: ___

What are you grateful for today?

_____
_____
_____

How are you feeling?

Monthly Reflection

"All your dreams can come true if you have the courage to pursue them." Walt Disney

What was your best experience for the month?

_____

_____

_____

What was your worst experience for the month?

_____

_____

_____

What were you mostly grateful for this month?

_____

_____

_____

What can I do to improve myself this month?

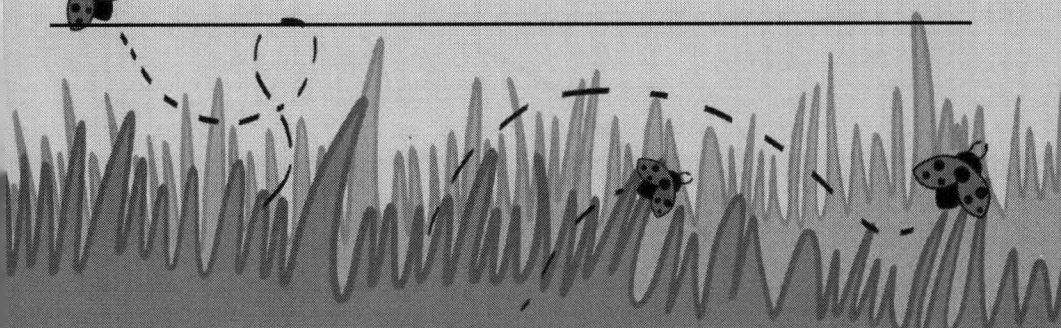

_____

_____

_____

"Mistakes are part of the dues one pays for a full life." Sophia Loren

Month: _____

Week: ___

What are you grateful for today?

_____

_____

_____

Week: ___

What are you grateful for today?

_____

_____

_____

Week: ___

What are you grateful for today?

_____

_____

_____

Week: ___

What are you grateful for today?

_____

_____

_____

How are you feeling?

Monthly Reflection

"Get busy living or get busy dying." Stephen King

What was your best experience for the month?

_____

_____

_____

What was your worst experience for the month?

_____

_____

_____

What were you mostly grateful for this month?

_____

_____

_____

What can I do to improve myself this month?

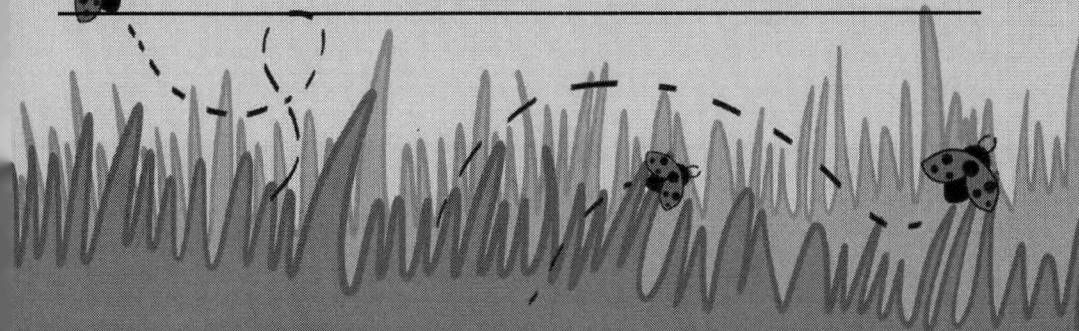

_____

_____

_____

"It always seems impossible until it is done."
Nelson Mandela

Month: _____

Week: ___

What are you grateful for today?

_____
_____
_____

Week: ___

What are you grateful for today?

_____
_____
_____

Week: ___

What are you grateful for today?

_____
_____
_____

Week: ___

What are you grateful for today?

_____
_____
_____

How are you feeling?

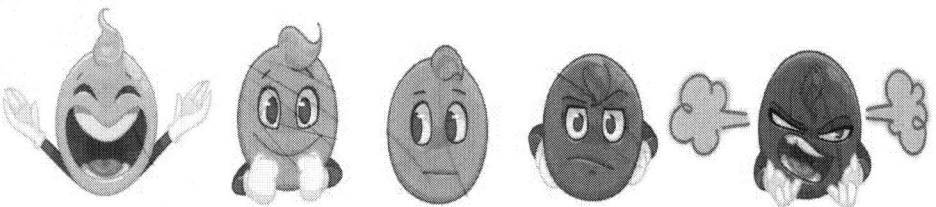

Monthly Reflection

"A successful man is one who can lay a firm foundation with the bricks others have thrown at him." David Brinkley

What was your best experience for the month?

_____

_____

_____

What was your worst experience for the month?

_____

_____

_____

What were you mostly grateful for this month?

_____

_____

_____

What can I do to improve myself this month?

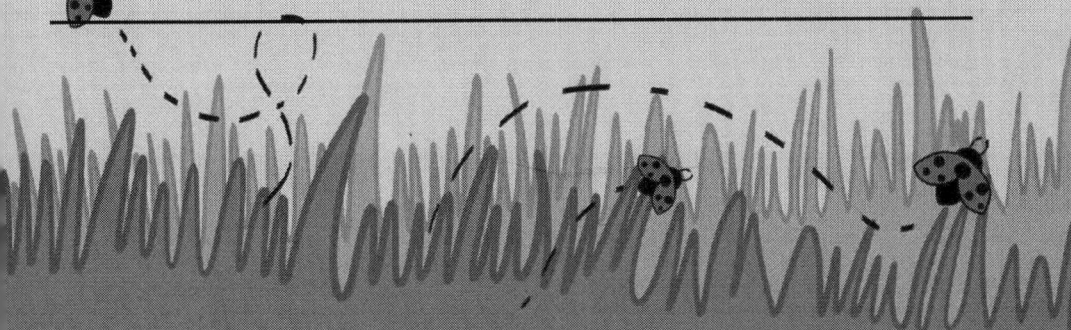

_____

_____

_____

"Do your own thing on your own terms and get what you came here for." Oliver James

Month: _____

Week: ___

What are you grateful for today?

_____
_____
_____

Week: ___

What are you grateful for today?

_____
_____
_____

Week: ___

What are you grateful for today?

_____
_____
_____

Week: ___

What are you grateful for today?

_____
_____
_____

How are you feeling?

Monthly Reflection

"I'm a success today because I had a friend who believed in me and I didn't have the heart to let him down." Abraham Lincoln

What was your best experience for the month?

_____

_____

_____

What was your worst experience for the month?

_____

_____

_____

What were you mostly grateful for this month?

_____

_____

_____

What can I do to improve myself this month?

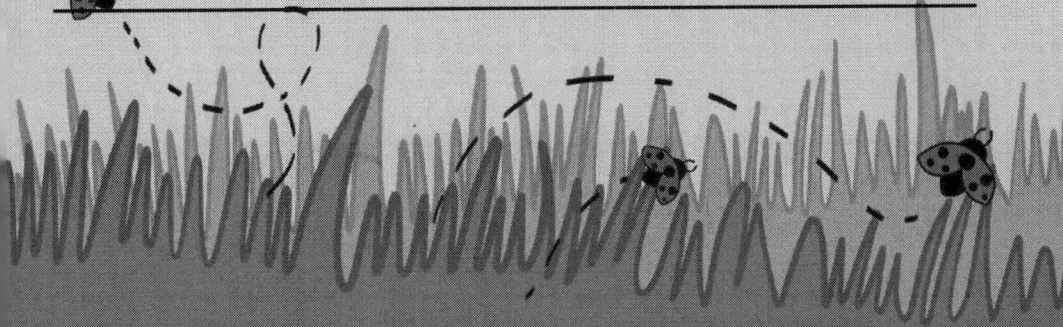

_____

_____

_____

"Do what you feel in your heart to be right, for you'll be criticized anyway." Eleanor Roosevelt

Month: _____

Week: ___

What are you grateful for today?

_____
_____
_____

Week: ___

What are you grateful for today?

_____
_____
_____

Week: ___

What are you grateful for today?

_____
_____
_____

Week: ___

What are you grateful for today?

_____
_____
_____

How are you feeling?

Monthly Reflection

"It had long since come to my attention that people of accomplishment rarely sat back and let things happen to them. They went out and happened to things." Leonardo Da Vinci

What was your best experience for the month?

_____

_____

_____

What was your worst experience for the month?

_____

_____

_____

What were you mostly grateful for this month?

_____

_____

_____

What can I do to improve myself this month?

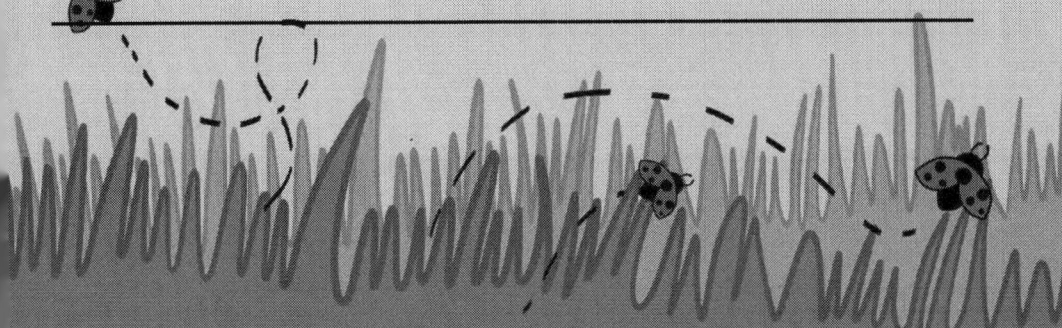

_____

_____

_____

"Whenever you find yourself on the majority, it's time to pause and reflect." Mark Twain

Month: _____

Week: ___

What are you grateful for today?

_____
_____
_____

Week: ___

What are you grateful for today?

_____
_____
_____

Week: ___

What are you grateful for today?

_____
_____
_____

Week: ___

What are you grateful for today?

_____
_____
_____

How are you feeling?

Monthly Reflection

"If you want to be happy, be." Leo Tolstoy

What was your best experience for the month?

_____

_____

_____

What was your worst experience for the month?

_____

_____

_____

What were you mostly grateful for this month?

_____

_____

_____

What can I do to improve myself this month?

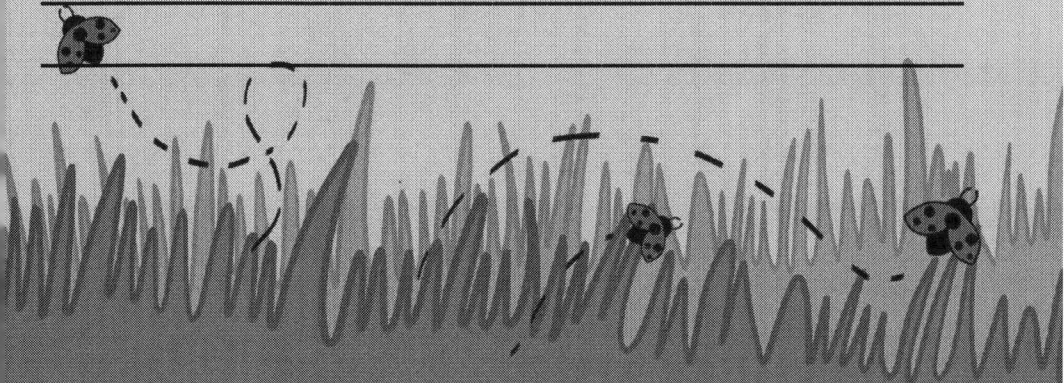

_____

_____

_____

"Great minds discuss ideas; average minds discuss events; small minds discuss people."
Eleanor Roosevelt

Month: _____

Week: ___

What are you grateful for today?

_____
_____
_____

Week: ___

What are you grateful for today?

_____
_____
_____

Week: ___

What are you grateful for today?

_____
_____
_____

Week: ___

What are you grateful for today?

_____
_____
_____

How are you feeling?

Monthly Reflection

"The No. 1 reason people fail in life is because they listen to their friends, family, and neighbors." Napoleon Hill

What was your best experience for the month?

_____

_____

_____

What was your worst experience for the month?

_____

_____

_____

What were you mostly grateful for this month?

_____

_____

_____

What can I do to improve myself this month?

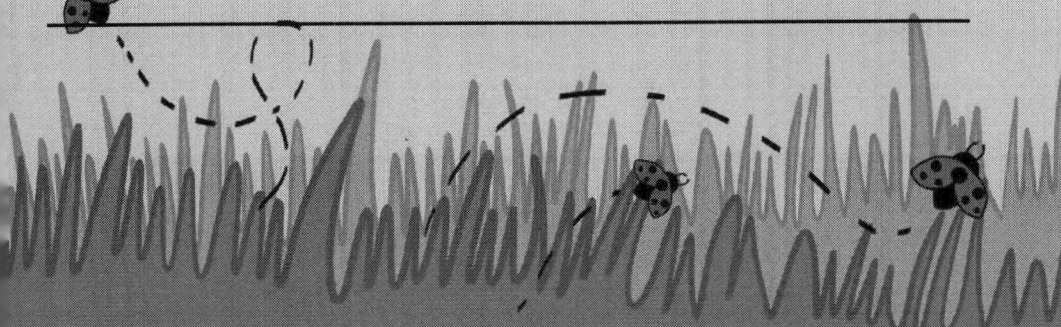

_____

_____

_____

"Those who dare to fail miserably can achieve greatly." John F. Kennedy

Month: _____

Week: ____

What are you grateful for today?

_____
_____
_____

Week: ____

What are you grateful for today?

_____
_____
_____

Week: ____

What are you grateful for today?

_____
_____
_____

Week: ____

What are you grateful for today?

_____
_____
_____

How are you feeling?

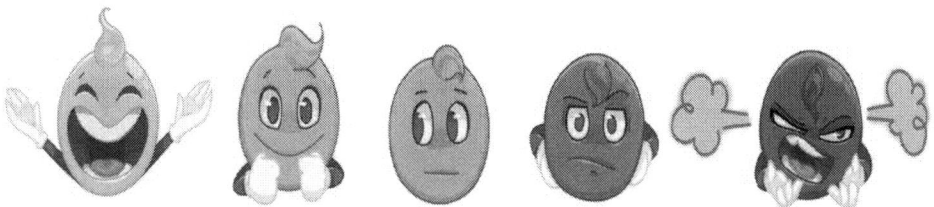

Monthly Reflection

"Success is not final; failure is not fatal: it is the courage to continue that counts." Winston Churchill

What was your best experience for the month?

_____

_____

_____

What was your worst experience for the month?

_____

_____

_____

What were you mostly grateful for this month?

_____

_____

_____

What can I do to improve myself this month?

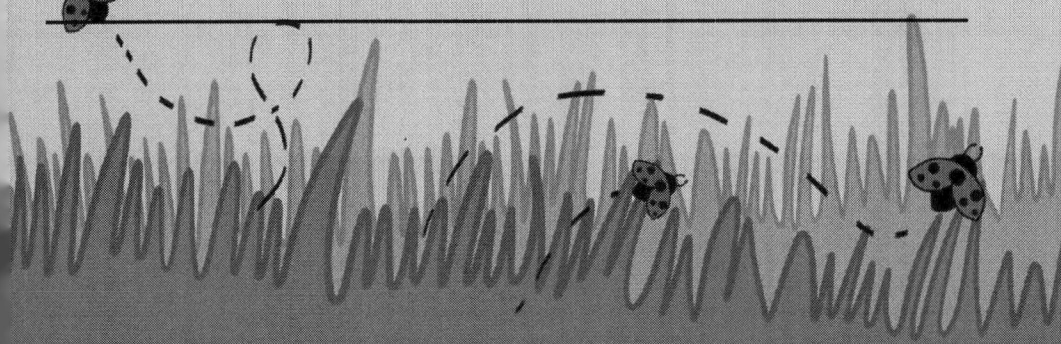

_____

_____

_____

"You only live once, but if you do it right, once is enough." Mae West

Month: _____

Week: ____

What are you grateful for today?

_____
_____
_____

Week: ____

What are you grateful for today?

_____
_____
_____

Week: ____

What are you grateful for today?

_____
_____
_____

Week: ____

What are you grateful for today?

_____
_____
_____

How are you feeling?

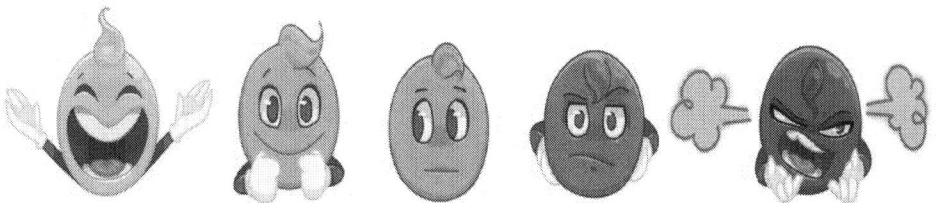

Monthly Reflection

.*"The whole secret of a successful life is to find out what is one's destiny to do, and then do it."* Henry Ford

What was your best experience for the month?

_____

_____

_____

What was your worst experience for the month?

_____

_____

_____

What were you mostly grateful for this month?

_____

_____

_____

What can I do to improve myself this month?

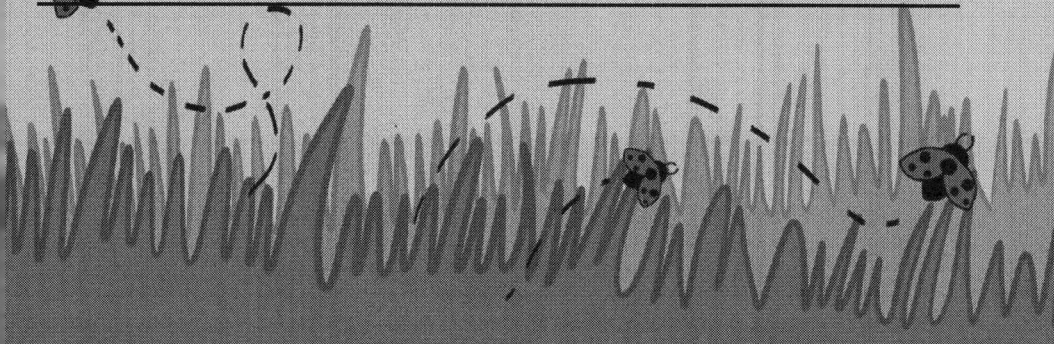

_____

_____

_____

"He that falls in love with himself will have no rivals." Benjamin Franklin

Month: _____

Week: ___

What are you grateful for today?

_____
_____
_____

Week: ___

What are you grateful for today?

_____
_____
_____

Week: ___

What are you grateful for today?

_____
_____
_____

Week: ___

What are you grateful for today?

_____
_____
_____

How are you feeling?

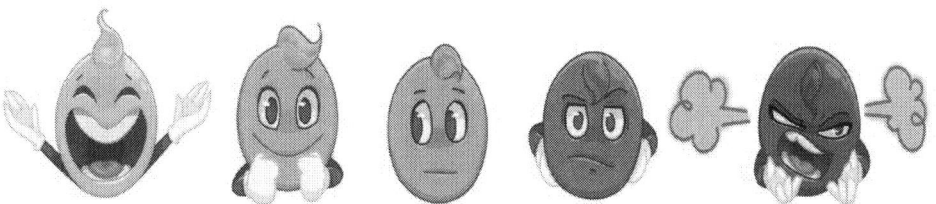

Monthly Reflection

"It is hard to fail, but it's worse never to have tried to success."
Theodore Roosevelt

What was your best experience for the month?

_____

_____

_____

What was your worst experience for the month?

_____

_____

_____

What were you mostly grateful for this month?

_____

_____

_____

What can I do to improve myself this month?

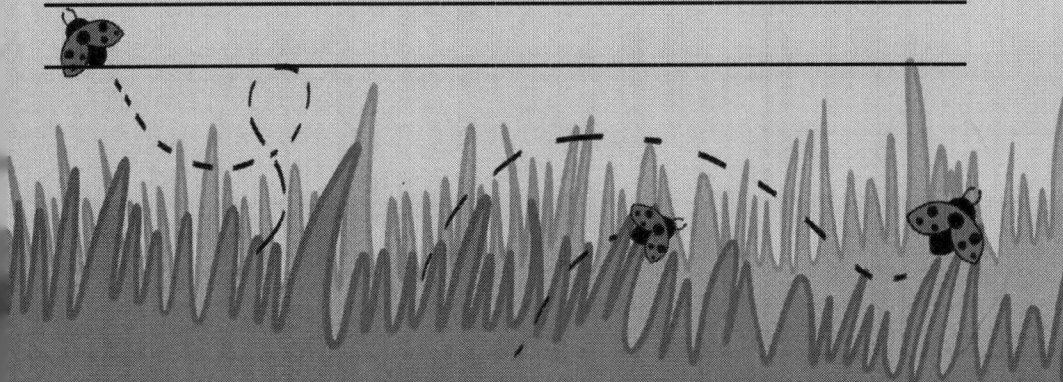

_____

_____

"Let us always meet each other with smile, for the smile is the beginning of love."
Mother Theresa

Month: _____

Week: ___

What are you grateful for today?

_____
_____
_____

Week: ___

What are you grateful for today?

_____
_____
_____

Week: ___

What are you grateful for today?

_____
_____
_____

Week: ___

What are you grateful for today?

_____
_____
_____

How are you feeling?

Monthly Reflection

"Challenges are what make life interesting and overcoming them is what makes life meaningful." Joshua J. Marine

What was your best experience for the month?

_____

_____

_____

What was your worst experience for the month?

_____

_____

_____

What were you mostly grateful for this month?

_____

_____

_____

What can I do to improve myself this month?

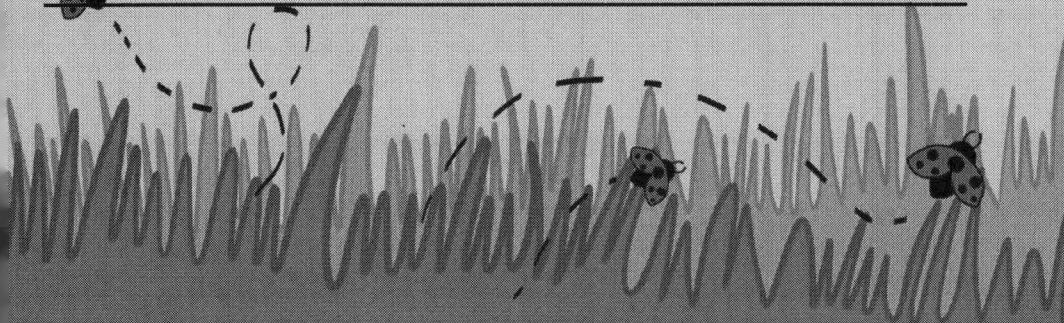

_____

_____

_____

"Our greatest fear should not be of failure, but of succeeding at things in life that don't really matter." Francis Chan

Month: _____

Week: ____

What are you grateful for today?

_____
_____
_____

Week: ____

What are you grateful for today?

_____
_____
_____

Week: ____

What are you grateful for today?

_____
_____
_____

Week: ____

What are you grateful for today?

_____
_____
_____

How are you feeling?

ACTIVITY

Create your own affirmations.

_____

_____

_____

_____

_____

_____

_____

_____

_____

_____

ACTIVITY

What is my purpose?

_____
_____
_____
_____
_____
_____
_____
_____

Who do I want to be?

_____
_____
_____
_____
_____
_____
_____
_____
_____

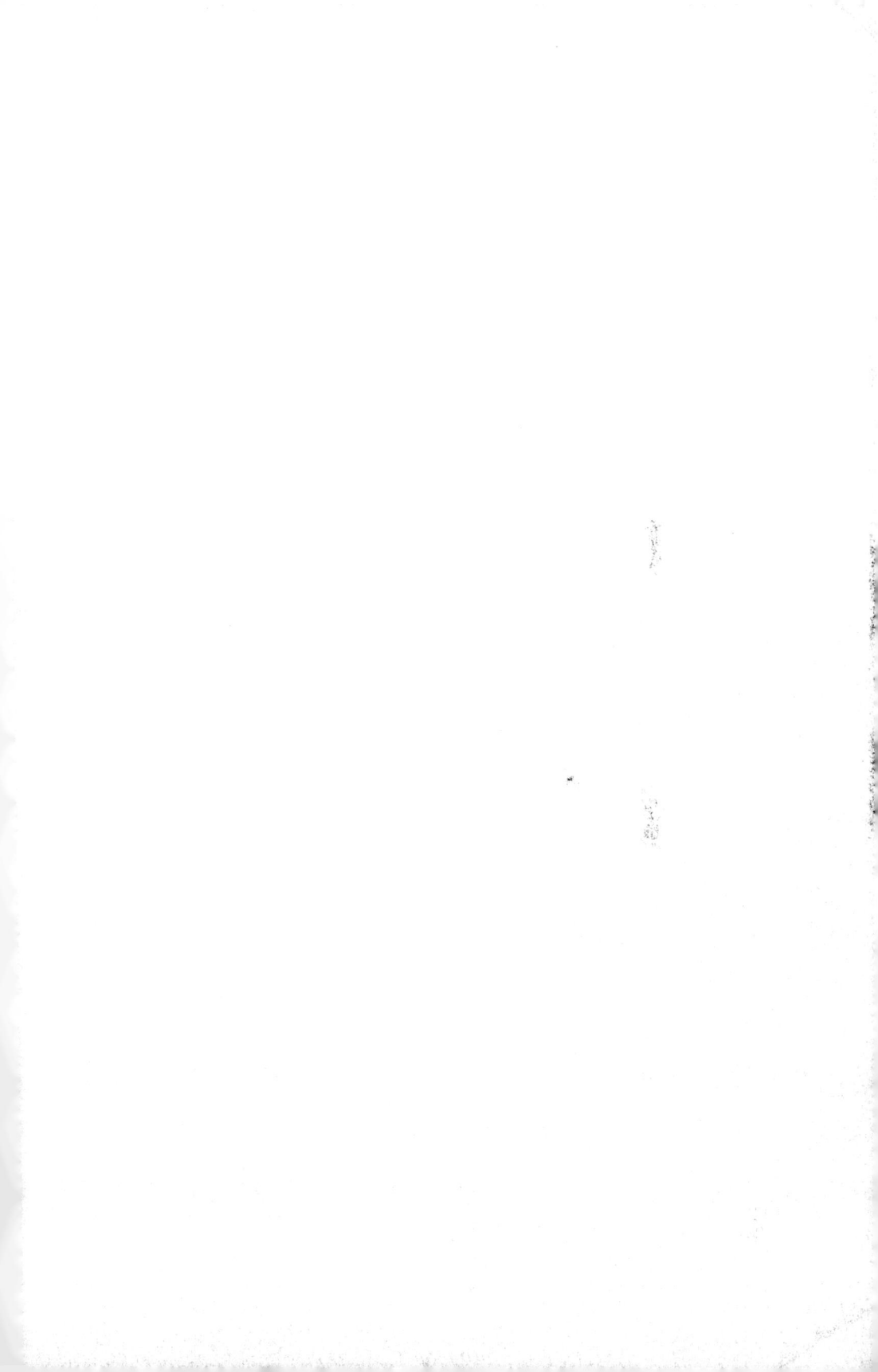

Made in the USA
Columbia, SC
05 January 2020